SPECTRUM®
EARLY YEARS

Basic Beginnings
SAME &
DIFFERENT

Published by Spectrum®
an imprint of Carson-Dellosa Publishing LLC
Greensboro, NC

Spectrum
An imprint of Carson-Dellosa Publishing, LLC
P.O. Box 35665
Greensboro, NC 27425-5665

carsondellosa.com

ISBN 978-1-60996-888-5   01-044127844

Table of Contents

Welcome to *Basic Beginnings*

Basic Beginnings is a creative and developmentally appropriate series designed to fuel your child's learning potential. The early years of your child's life are bursting with cognitive and physical development. Therefore, it is essential to prepare your child for the basic skills and fine motor skills that are emphasized in the 21st century classroom. Basic skills include concepts such as recognizing letters, numbers, colors, shapes, and identifying same, different, and sequences of events. Fine motor skills are movements produced by small muscles or muscle groups, such as the precise hand movements required to write, cut, glue, and color. A child in preschool spends a lot of his or her day developing these muscles.

Basic Beginnings approaches learning through a developmentally appropriate process—ensuring your child is building the best foundation possible for preschool. Each activity is unique and fun, and stimulates your child's fine motor skills, hand-eye coordination, and ability to follow directions. Help your child complete the activities in this book. Each activity includes simple, step-by-step instructions. Provide your child with pencils, crayons, scissors, and glue for the various and creative activities he or she is about to discover.

Each book also includes three cutout mini books that reinforce the concepts your child is learning. You and your child will enjoy reading these simple stories together. Your child can make each story his or her own by coloring it, cutting it out, and, with your help, stapling the story together. Allow him or her to share the stories with you and others. Your child will begin to recognize sight words, hear vowel sounds, and understand sequences of events as he or she shares these delightful stories. With *Basic Beginnings*, the learning is never confined to the pages!

Introduction to *Same & Different*

Visual discrimination is the ability to effectively use your eyes to discern and interpret visual information. A young child needs practice with fun activities to help him or her learn how to accurately interpret what he or she is seeing. Accurate visual perception is crucial to understanding the world around us. A child needs to see details in the environment, which ultimately leads to the ability to discriminate between various numerals and alphabet letters. The activities in *Same & Different* will help your child develop these skills.

Each activity comes with its own specific directions. Parents should carefully read the directions and make sure their child clearly understands them. If your child does not understand the concepts presented in each activity, he or she is not going to understand what he or she is supposed to look for. For example, if a child is supposed to be visually discriminating things that are the same, they must understand the concept of same to complete the activity. If your child needs some demonstrations of these concepts, see the activities below for fun and interactive ways to assist your child in learning—before he or she attempts the visual discrimination activities in this workbook.

Mix and Match Shoes

Have your child collect several pairs of shoes (or socks) and place them in a pile. Ask your child to collect one shoe at a time and set it aside. As your child collects each shoe, ask him or her to place shoes that are the same together. Then, once all the shoes are matched up, ask your child to switch the pairs of shoes around. Explain that the shoes are now different from each other. Allow your child to mix and match shoes until the meaning of same and different is understood.

What Does Not Belong?

On a tabletop, place three objects that should go together and one object that does not belong. In order to make this a concrete activity for your child, use real objects not pictures. For example: three toy cars and a crayon; three crayons and a pencil; three cups and a plate; three blocks and scissors, and so on. Your child will be able to see the connection between the objects, and identify which object does not belong.

Hide and Seek

This activity is not the typical "hide and seek" game. First, hide a small object while your child is out of the room. Then, tell your child the name of the object missing and allow your child to search the room to find it. Do not place the object behind or under anything. Place the object in clear view, but have it in a place where the object usually would not be found, such as a small car on a bookshelf. You can hide several objects in one game.

Developmental Checklist

Between Ages of Two and Three:

- ☐ Imitates circular scribble and horizontal and vertical lines
- ☐ Builds a tower of 6 blocks
- ☐ Holds crayon with thumb and fingers (not fist)
- ☐ Snips with scissors
- ☐ Puts tiny objects in small containers
- ☐ Folds paper in half
- ☐ Pulls toys with strings
- ☐ Strings 1 to 4 large beads
- ☐ Uses a spoon
- ☐ Turns single pages of a book
- ☐ One hand begins to be dominant
- ☐ Paints with some wrist action
- ☐ Pounds, rolls, pulls, and squeezes play dough

Between Ages of Three and Four:

- ☐ Builds a tower of 9 blocks
- ☐ Snips with scissors
- ☐ Completes a 5–6 piece puzzle
- ☐ Holds a crayon with three fingers
- ☐ Copies a circle
- ☐ Copies vertical and horizontal lines
- ☐ Draws a person with a head
- ☐ Uses a spoon and fork with little spillage
- ☐ Opens rotating door handles
- ☐ Strings ½ inch beads
- ☐ Traces a square
- ☐ Unzips separating zipper; zips and unzips non-separating zipper
- ☐ Unbuttons large and small buttons
- ☐ Identifies body parts

Between Ages of Four and Five:

- ☐ Builds a tower of 10 blocks
- ☐ Strings ¼ inch beads
- ☐ Scissor skills improved – cuts on lines and cuts simple shapes

- ☐ Copies a cross and a square
- ☐ Can independently button and unbutton
- ☐ Uses dominant hand with better coordination
- ☐ Able to do 6–10 piece puzzles
- ☐ Can print some uppercase letters
- ☐ Draws a person with 2 to 4 body parts
- ☐ Holds writing tools with three fingers – control increasing
- ☐ Dresses and undresses independently – managing buttons and zippers
- ☐ No longer switches hands in the middle of an activity
- ☐ Builds a 6 block pyramid

Between Ages of Five and Six:

- ☐ Bounces and catches balls
- ☐ Builds a tower of 12 blocks
- ☐ Can build 3 steps from 6 blocks
- ☐ Draws angles, triangles, and other geometric shapes
- ☐ Draws a complete person with a head, body, legs, arms, and a face
- ☐ Can color within lines
- ☐ Cutting skills improved – can cut along lines and can cut out a circle
- ☐ Holds a knife in the dominant hand
- ☐ Copies first name
- ☐ Has mastered an adult grasp of a pencil
- ☐ Hand dominance is well-established
- ☐ Can use glue appropriately
- ☐ Prints numerals 1 to 5
- ☐ Enjoys working with a variety of mediums: paint, clay, glitter, chalk, glue, etc.
- ☐ Begins to tie shoes
- ☐ Can "sew" lacing cards
- ☐ Completes a 12–15 piece puzzle
- ☐ Learning how to print upper- and lowercase letters

Same & Different

Go-Togethers

Directions: Draw lines to connect the things that go together.

7

Match the Same

Directions: Name each animal. Draw a line to match each animal that is the same.

Connect the Fish

Directions: Draw a line to match the fish that are the same.

Connect the Turtles

Directions: Draw a line to match the turtles that are the same.

Same & Different

Same Foods

Directions: Circle the foods that are the same.

Same & Different

Same Vehicles

Directions: Circle each vehicle that is the same.

Same & Different

Baby Animals

Directions: Color the baby animals that are the same.

Same Bugs

Directions: Color the bugs that are the same.

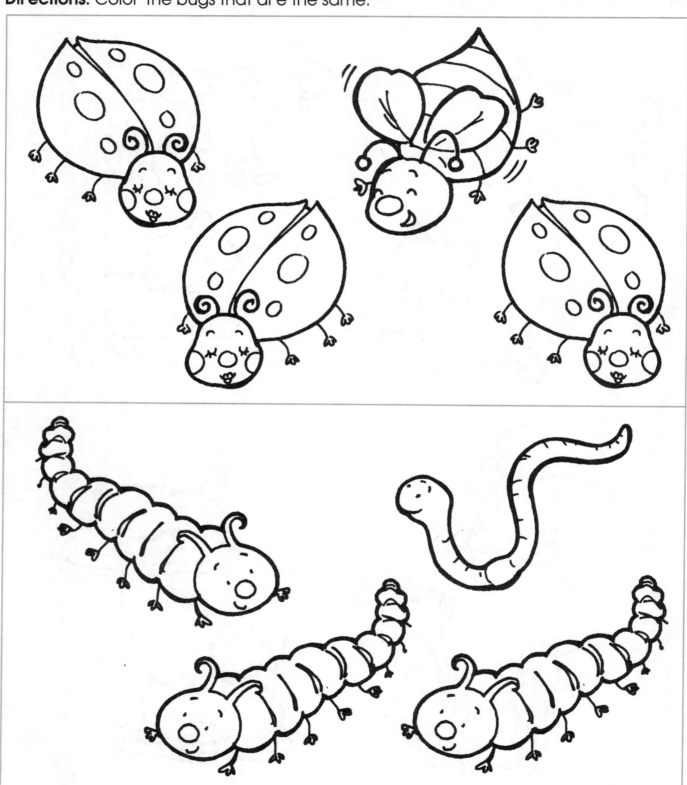

Same & Different

Three Little Kittens

Directions: Say the rhyme "The Three Little Kittens." The kittens are crying because they lost their mittens. Draw a line to match the mittens to the correct kitten.

15

Same

Directions: Color the things that are the same in each row.

Same & Different

Pig Pen Families

Directions: Look at the pigs. How are they different? Cut out the baby pigs below. Glue each set of baby pigs by its matching mother.

17

Same & Different

2

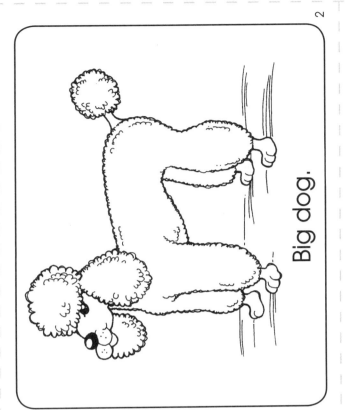

Big dog.

4

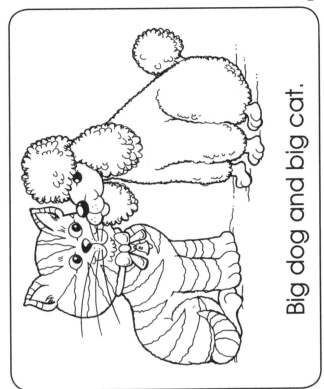

Big dog and big cat.

1

Big Cat and Little Dog

3

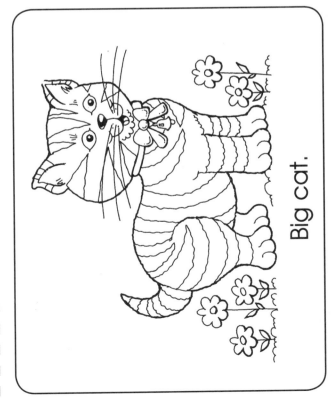

Big cat.

Same & Different

6

Little cat.

8

Directions: Draw a line to match the words that are the same.

little   and

big   little

big

and

Directions: First, ask your child to color the mini book. Then, help him or her cut along the dotted lines. Next, have your child arrange the pages in the correct order. Staple the pages together. Read the story out loud to your child.

Extension ideas:
1. Ask your child to draw a big dog and little cat. Tell a story about them.

5

Little dog.

7

Little dog and big cat.

Same & Different

What's Different?

Directions: Color the picture that is different in each row.

23

Same & Different

Things that Fly

Directions: Draw an **X** on the picture that is different in each row.

Same & Different

Things that Swim

Directions: Draw an **X** on the picture that is different in each row.

25

Which Person is Different?

Directions: Color the person that is different in each row.

Same & Different

Which Dog is Different?

Directions: Draw an **X** over the dog that is different.

27

Wrong Baby!

Directions: Draw an **X** on the baby that does not belong.

Same & Different

Which is Wrong?

Directions: Color the animal that is different.

29

Same & Different

Circles

Directions: Trace the circles.

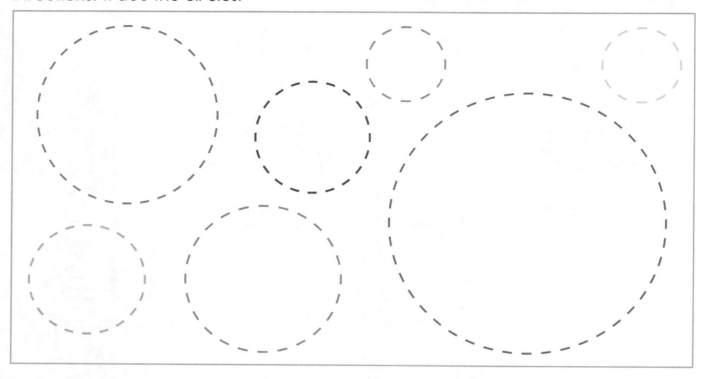

Directions: Color the pictures that are the same shape as a circle. Draw an **X** on the pictures that are different.

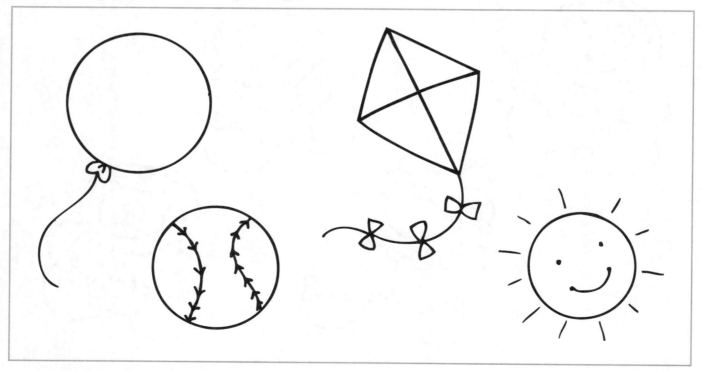

Same & Different

Squares

Directions: Trace the squares.

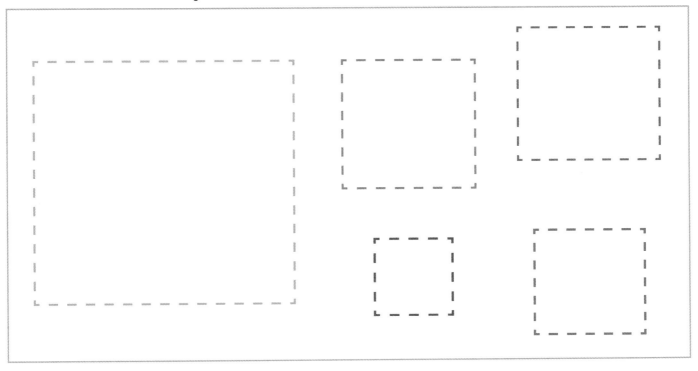

Directions: Color the shapes that are the same as a square **blue**. Color shapes that are different **red**.

Same & Different

Triangles

Directions: Trace the triangles.

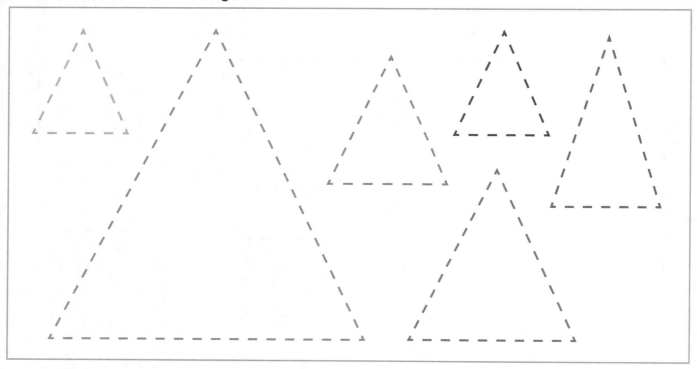

Directions: Draw an **X** on the pictures that are not the same shape as a triangle.
Circle the pictures that are the same.

Same & Different

Rectangles

Directions: Trace the rectangles.

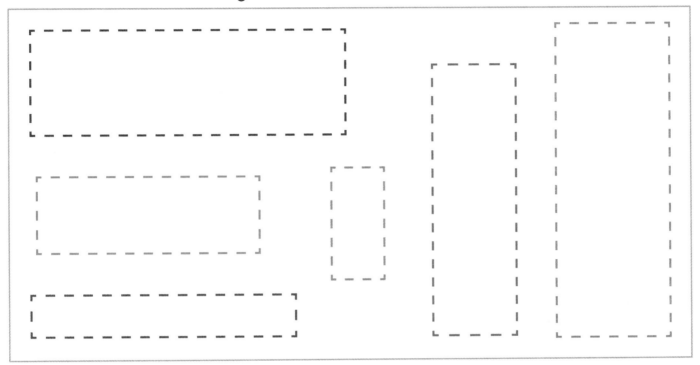

Directions: Color the shapes that are the same as a rectangle **purple**. Color shapes that are different **green**.

33

Rhombuses

Directions: Trace the rhombuses.

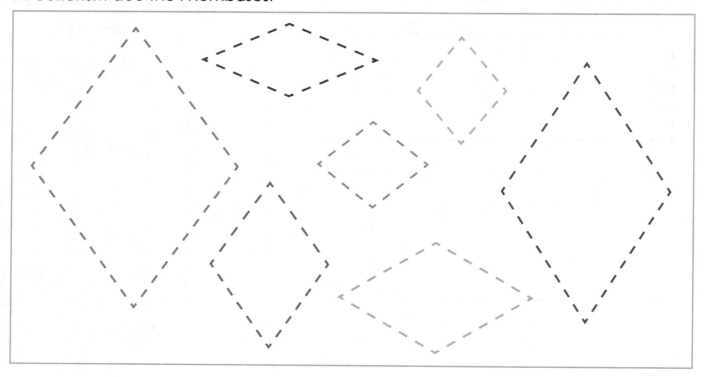

Directions: Color the pictures that are the same shape as a rhombus. Draw an **X** on the pictures that are different.

Stars

Directions: Trace the stars.

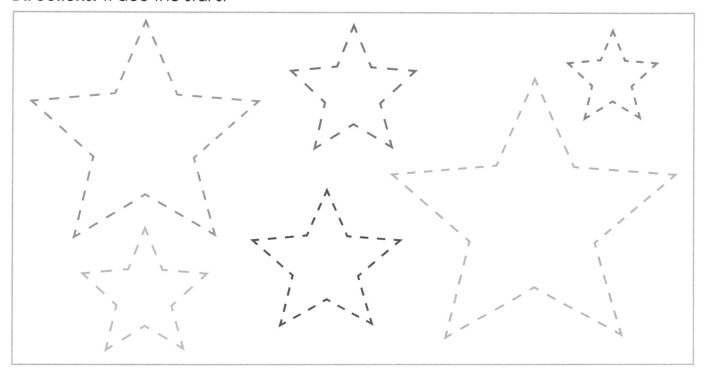

Directions: Color the shapes that are the same as a star yellow. Color shapes that
are different pink.

Same & Different

Ovals

Directions: Trace the ovals.

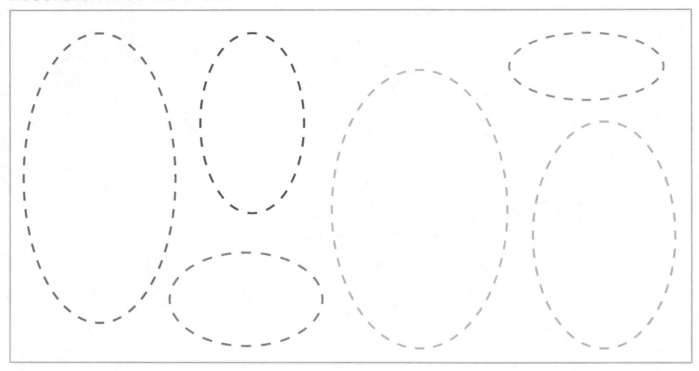

Directions: Color the pictures that are the same shape as an oval. Draw an **X** on the pictures that are different.

Same & Different

Octagons

Directions: Trace the octagons.

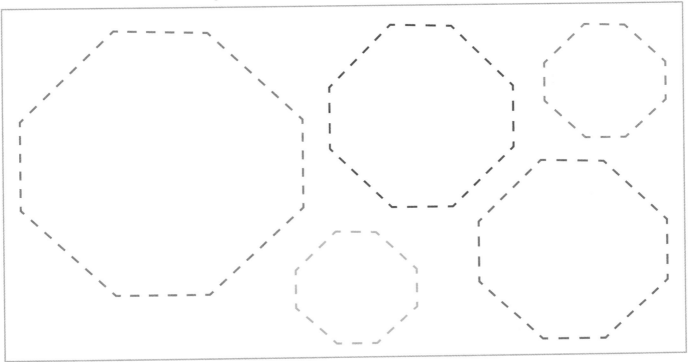

Directions: Color the shapes that are the same as an octagon **red**. Color shapes that are different **brown**.

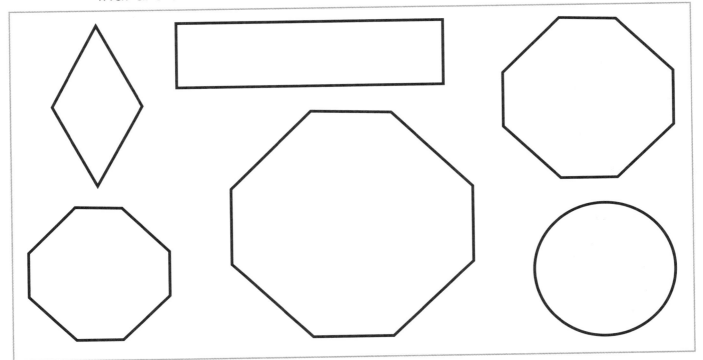

Match the Shapes!

Directions: Draw lines to match the shapes that are the same. Color.

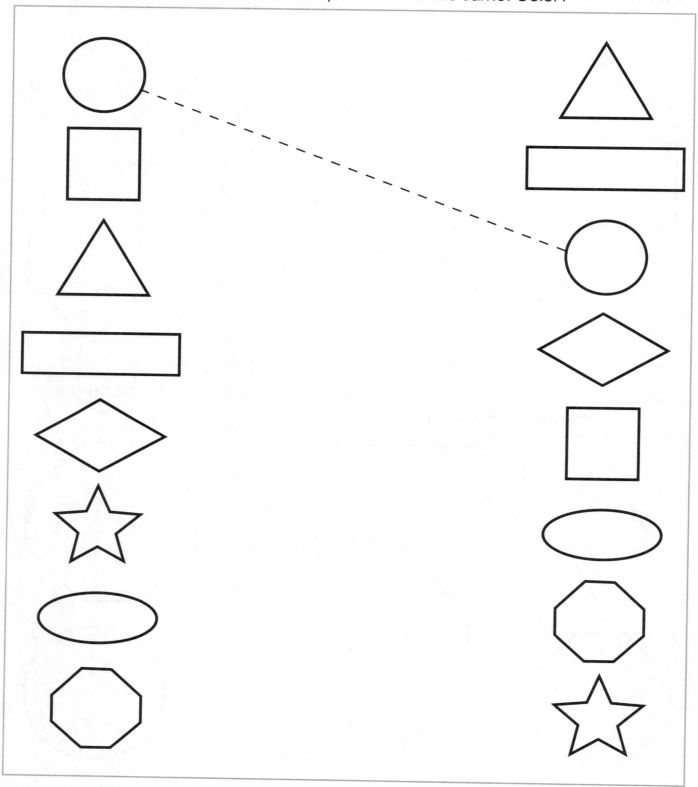

Same & Different

2

The little dog and
the big cat like to run.

4

Come here big cat.
Come here little dog.

1

Little Dog and
Big Cat Play

3

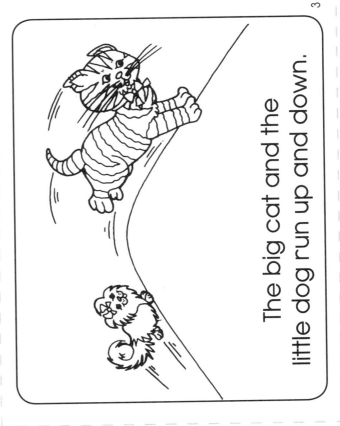

The big cat and the
little dog run up and down.

39

6

Come and run and play.

8

Directions: First, ask your child to color the mini book. Then, help him or her cut along the dotted lines. Next, have your child arrange the pages in the correct order. Staple the pages together. Read the story out loud to your child.

Look at Big Cat and Little Dog. Ask your child how they are different? The same?

5

I can run with you.

7

I like to run and play with little dog and big cat.

Same & Different

Colorful Shapes

Directions: Color all the shapes that are the same.

43

Same & Different

Bead Patterns

Directions: Look at the beads. Color the bead that should come next.

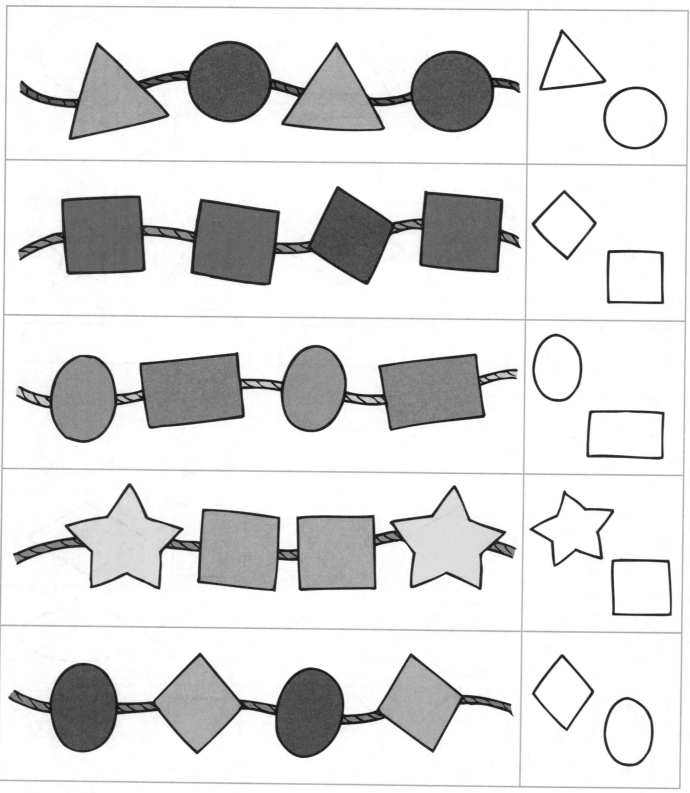

Same & Different

What's Missing?

Directions: Look at the two turtles. Use your pencil to make the second turtle the same as the first. Then, color both turtles.

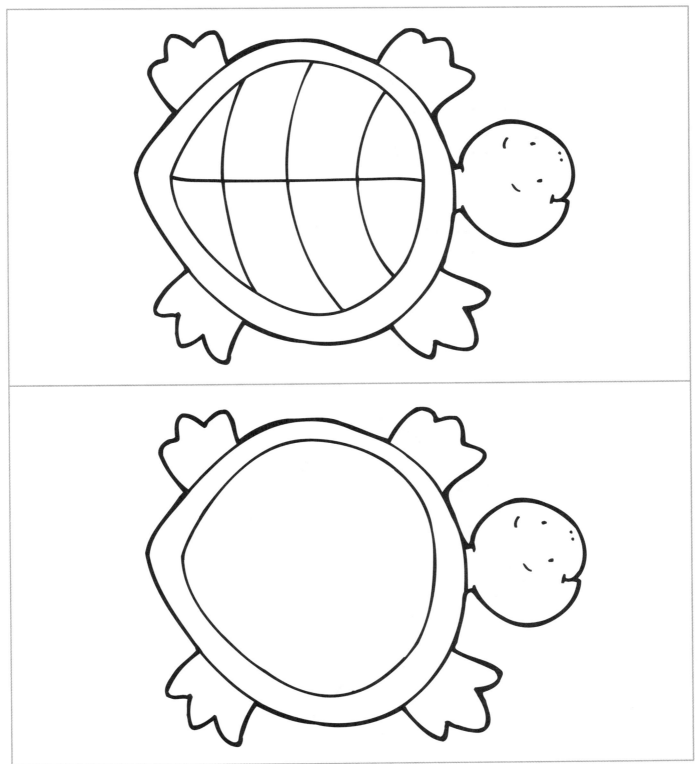

45

Help the Bugs!

Directions: Look at each bug. They are missing something. Add the missing body parts to each bug. Then, color the bugs.

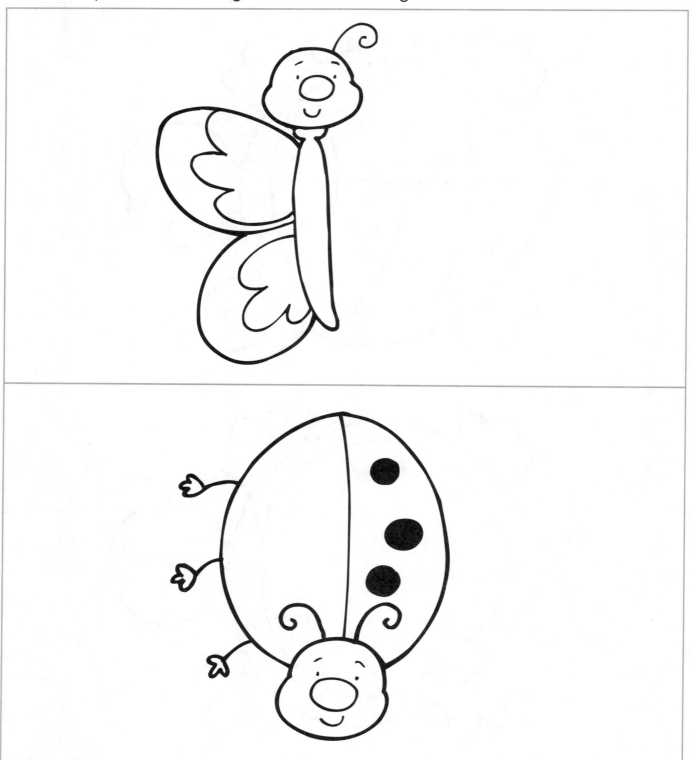

Same & Different

Splish & Splash

Directions: Look at the penguins. They are the same. Draw and color each penguin
to make it different.

Sunflowers

Directions: Look at each sunflower. They are the same. Make them different. Color one sunflower yellow. Draw a bumblebee on another. Color the rest any way you like.

48   *Same & Different*

Over and Under the Rainbow

Directions: Cut out the birds and pot of gold below. Glue the pot of gold under the rainbow. Glue the birds over the rainbow.

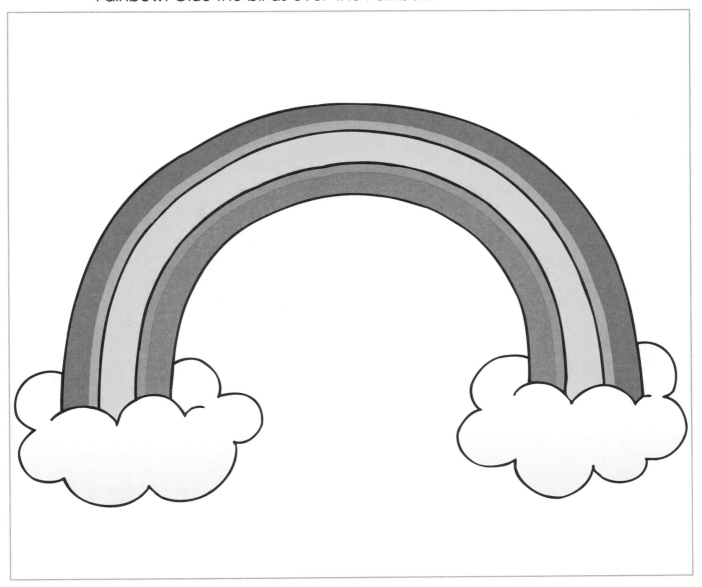

Same & Different

Top and Bottom Refrigerator

Directions: Cut out the pictures below. Glue the things you drink on the top shelf. Glue the things you eat on the bottom shelf.

Same & Different

Up and Down Climbing

Directions: Cut out the pictures below. Glue the monkey climbing up the tree. Glue the lizard climbing down the tree.

53

Up and Down

I am up.

I am up.

I am down.

I am down.

Up and down. Up and down.

6

Directions: Draw a line to match the words that are the same.

up   am

am   down

down   up

Directions: First, ask your child to color the mini book. Then, help him or her cut along the dotted lines. Next, have your child arrange the pages in the correct order. Staple the pages together. Read the story out loud to your child.

5

I am down.

Down! Down! Down!

7

Same & Different

What's Wrong at the Beach?

Directions: Look carefully at the beach. Circle the things that should not be happening at the beach. Color the picture.

59

What's Missing at School?

Directions: Look at **Picture 1**. Then, look at **Picture 2**. They are not the same. There are five things missing in **Picture 2**. Find and color the items in **Picture 1** that are missing in **Picture 2**.

Picture 1

Picture 2

These are the missing items: *the flag in the window, the apple on the teacher's desk, the stripes on the middle boy's shirt, the pencil in the last girl's hand, and the clock.*

60

Same & Different

What's Missing by the Pond?

Directions: Look at **Picture 1**. Then, look at **Picture 2**. They are not the same. There are five things missing in **Picture 2**. Find and color the items in **Picture 1** that are missing in **Picture 2**.

Picture 1

Picture 2

These are the missing items: *one of the baby ducks, the beaver's tail, the leaping frog, the flying bug, and the weeds by the lily pad.*

Same & Different

Fun in the Snow

Directions: Look at **Picture 1**. Then, look at **Picture 2**. They are not the same. There are six things missing in **Picture 2**. Find and circle the items in **Picture 1** that are missing in **Picture 2**.

Picture 1

Picture 2

These are the missing items: *bird on the bucket of coal, the rabbit, the mouse, the snowman's stick arm, the flower on the snowman's hat, and the tree by the house.*

62

Same & Different

At the Lake

Directions: Look at **Picture 1**. Then, look at **Picture 2**. They are not the same. There are six things missing in **Picture 2**. Draw the missing items in **Picture 2**.

Picture 1

Picture 2

These are the missing items: *the cloud, the girl by the water with pigtails, sunglasses, two trees, flower on girl's swimsuit, and the small umbrella by the chair.*

Same & Different

Playing Outside

Directions: Look at **Picture 1**. Then, look at **Picture 2**. They are not the same. There are five things missing in **Picture 2**. Find and color the items in **Picture 1** that are missing in **Picture 2**.

Picture 1

Picture 2

These are the missing items: *the dog between the trees, the bird on the swingset, the ball, the sun, and the birdbath.*

Same & Different